RED

RED

GEORGE
ELLIOTT
CLARKE

GASPEREAU
PRESS MMXI

For William Lloyd Clarke (1935–2005)
Father, Artist, Motorcyclist, Intellectual,
Liberal, Idealist, Actor, Romantic.

I stop there, for who can tell me what beauty is?
FRANTZ FANON

Beauty must never be explained.
EZRA POUND

SEEING RED

RED *a. & n. 1. a.* of or approaching the colour seen at least-refracted end of spectrum, of shades varying from crimson to bright brown and orange, esp. those seen in blood, rubies, glowing coals, human lips, and fox's hair, (*red as a rose* etc.; *blood, fiery, yellowish, deep*, etc., *-red*)....

THE CONCISE OXFORD DICTIONARY:
NEW EDITION

Blue (2001) and *Black* (2006) constitute my 'colouring' books—or so I like to think, where I try various forms and strike different (rhetorical) poses. While drafting this fresh, shady collection, *Red* flared up, at once, as *the* choice—*scarlet*—title letters....

Part-Aboriginal, I must be a *noir "peau rouge."* Shadowing Mao's poetics and Detroit Red's philosophy, my politics also shade rose-tinted.

Herein sue Redskin, black-mouth blues. Likely—or not....

GEORGE ELLIOTT CLARKE, NISAN XI

RED LETTERS

Upon occasion we can see beauty in disease,
or beauty in the sinister, beauty even in the ugly.

NORMAN MAILER

RED HAND

Will all great Neptune's ocean wash this blood
Clean from my hand? No, this my hand will rather
The multitudinous seas incarnadine,
Making the green one red.

MACBETH, II.iii.64–67

To the Poet †

Poet! Damn you if you crave public love!
People clap raucously, then, fickle, stop.
Fools don scholars' tassels, bray their critiques,
While crowds' hoorays chill—or scald—your marrow.
Best to stand Caesar-calm, statue-austere:
It's majesty, yes, to dwell defiant,
Castled in your own soul, free and aloof!
Perfect your flowers, distill their dream liqueurs,
But ignore all praise of your past confections.
Judge for yourself your vineyard's heady wine:
Your strict taste dictates its vintage sweetness!
Do you want joy? Let the pack bay and howl:
Let them snarl and spit on your altar's flames
And breathe your temple's triumphant perfumes!

† *Pace* Constance Garnett's translation of Alexander Pushkin's
Russian verse.

Creole Lyric

Like lightning, letters yield inklings of light.
Spy alphabet alba: italic blues.

Orchestrate every line with stern lilting:
Voice no Tin Pan ballads, no typecast tunes.

Beware all premature euphoria!
(Dust upon dust, word after word, defines failure.)

Dash down the poem, then dash away, crying.
Scribble tribal syllables in off-hand style.

When you are no more visible than your voice is now,
The cut and tuck of each line, tacking,
Will still compose a rampart from which arrows hit home.

Be extravagant and seize clarity,
Cadenced, alive with elegy, then turn
To papal silence: Until the page turns.

Angle

In poetry,
the hand
is also an eye—

you see
what I mean

as the pen leans
aslant the page—
agape—

a mouth,
speaking
what the hand says

you and I see....

Uta

This emphatic pen—
A roused viper—darts venom
Without antidote,
Indelibly poisonous—
Ink of cyanide and bile.

Other Angles

Red is the Côte d'Azur, the Black Sea, the Dead Sea
Red is goose-stepping gulls and overstepping dogs
Red is a bloody shit
Red: A tongue accustomed to corruption
A grievous stallion, unbridled in bed, charges, red
Red is an orangutan licking white snatch in the rue Morgue
Red is a severe poppy, a severed neck
The purple prose a blonde ejaculates in a blue movie gushes red
Red is the Moltke River black with gangrene weeds brushing the surface
Red is Pushkin's statue in St. Petersburg, Russia, mobbed by Haligonian
    sparrows and pigeons
The invisible brilliance of Hell defines red
Red is weather-beaten, worm-eaten stars
Red is *Black Label, Blue Label, Gold Label, Green Label, Red Label*
Piero Piccioni, Ennio Morricone, and Henry Mancini compose red
Red is Romania with plum blossoms and Greece with almond blossoms
(See *RED*, starring the resplendent, elegantly sexy Helen Mirren)
Red is a white lie illuminating a blackout
Red is a choir of hanged men
Red is this excellent Scotch I have put away
Red's the Orange Free State, the Yellow Peril, the Black Dahlia
Red is *La Café Soledad*, 100% pure coffee from Oaxaca, México
Red is Yellowknife, Whitehorse, Green Gables, and Red Deer
An unconvincing black and a phony white sound red
Red's an asinine bull studding a pig-headed bitch
Red is April, Libra, Aquarius, and July
Red is *Diamonds Are Forever For Your Eyes Only From Russia With Love*
    because *You Only Live Twice*
That library of burning books (definitely in Texas) ignited red

Red is *film noir*, a *giallo*, and a black comedy performed in whiteface mime
Red is suicidal survival
Red is *Tenzan* sake, Alc. Cont. 18%, in a bottle wrapped in rice paper
Screening *Blue Velvet* in Black September for Green Berets is awfully red
Red is fragrant flaming violet Klansmen barbecued on a blazing cross
Red is sun-blinded fog, gold hair over a white shirt
To be transcendentally black is red
Red is a wriggling, half-crushed fly
Red is Durrell's Rodos and its Rhodesian (or Lesbian) nudes
Thinking only about the white gal's tight ass is red
Red is the red-white-and-blue and the red-black-and-green
Red is Aboriginal and African and Chinese and Cuban and Nova Scotian
Red is *George & Rue*, *Illuminated Verses*, *Trudeau: Long March / Shining Path*, *Blues and Bliss*, *I & I*, and *Red*—
Poetry in the blood.

RED FACE

I'll gild the faces of the grooms withal,
For it must seem their guilt.†

MACBETH, II.iii.60–61

---

† "Gold was ordinarily spoken of as red." See *Macbeth:*
Texts and Contexts (1999), ed. William C. Carroll.

Forgotten Diatribe

You were not a traitor.
You were betrayed.
You were somebody.
You loved nobody.
You wrote to deadline and you lied on cue.
You lavished on the acid.
You thought *Beauty* a corruption of *booty*.
You swore, "She'll get her ticket punched."
You choked on your taxes.
You voted Tory accordingly.
You gushed fly-attractive honey.
You pushed shit.
You could degrade any republic quickly.
Your lines confused Austin C. Clarke with Arthur C. Clarke.
You were a poet—but with the poetry subtracted.
You threw back your head like a hungry pig.
You were not considered a rapist.
You corrupted Black English by cussing in French.
You liked to grovel in the dirt.
You were most comfortable there.
You were an expert castrator.
You always came away feeling nauseated.
You lapped up hard liquor greedily.
You got a wine-swollen, wine-fattened gut.
You abused alcohol and yourself.
You did disgusting things with your left hand.
Your body was whitened by metaphor.
You gleamed like a half-squashed cockroach.
You impounded the Pound-broken pentameter.

You twisted *ce lignum crucis* into *cunnilingus*.
　　　You were hurt by literature.
You slept with a shotgun cocked at your plush lips.
　　　You were awful laughable.
You had good reason to be ashamed.
　　　You shot yourself through your right eye.
Your body stank, maggot-rich, for weeks.
　　　You were a professional amnesiac.
But first you were forgotten.

Royal Audience

True: Dog-and-Bitch aristocrats
trot all tarted up, traditionally hideous,
despite tintinnabulation and twittering—
saccharine blather of the Press,

praising, appraising,
each luminous parasite
and their always trashy offspring:
Each face is counterfeit one spends (upon)

with sweaty, apish palm.
But *Il Principe* is especially, brutally pathetic:
He's the likeness of a mirror, shattered—
a clutch of pompous, bright infirmities.

See: The grisly creampuff, orthodox scumbag,
minces like a buttock whore,
pedestrian, trifling....
The seminal dastard simpers,

capering like a capon.
Il Duce is as bright as fresh, grey paint,
and parades a *papier-mâché* panache.
No, he is so waxen

that it's hard to get hold of an exact colour.
(He is white,
but needs more paint.)
His demeanour is as stale

as a spinster's virginity.
The immaculate imbecile—
his wit as difficult as chewing gum—
confuses my priestly garb

for the "dog collar" of a poetaster
spewing "doggerel."
I answered, "Never! Never!"
I now add, "Never! Never! Never!",

to curse his old health
à la Shakespeare:
Wagging tongue, then lapping shit,
he's disgusting even in his bones.

Okay: I don't mean to cut out the guts
of the guy:
Everyone knows
he's been in and out of the muck,

has known *commedia dell'arte* suffering.
It's not his fault his *pissoir* face
displays a mortician's pretty pallor,
sign of a moribund hierarchy.

Truly, it's his crudity
that makes me throw completely up.
A corrupt nothing,
his bio is *une sale histoire*,

an epistemology of feces—
incest that stinks of studs and sows,
of bastardy made right in the womb.
Here's one bit of good news:

The State taste for funerals.
Let The Prince perish into imperishable dust,
die extinguished, not distinguished,
and maggots eat him utterly to Hell,

so there's nothing left of him but thorns
in a nauseating cemetery.
Happily, his grave will prove a decorous quarantine,
preserving us from the contaminating function

of his every word, facial tic, and gesture,
those apt opportunities for disease.
Truth issues from my black mouth:
"Your Royal Highness, glisten always in excrement."

Autumnal

October-brutal rain batters down leaves.
Their mute hurt imitates an infirm whore
Dashed by a stroke—palsied, silenced, a bard
Emptied of words, who can only gesture,
Miming loud pain, no longer empowered
To gouge out bitter, irritating lines,
Succulently truculent.
                              Penitent
Leaves bloody the streets. Rain bangs down branches.
The sky slicks and glues itself upon us—
Slushing our opaque, snowy rhetoric.
            (Listen: Rainwater cries, "Red October!"
Perpetual, historical cata-
Strophe blushes or bleeds each leaf, born free
Then put down amid scarlet, raining ruin.)

Repulsion

The moon and the sun are assassins,
Murdering each other by turn.

Everywhere, daggers hit home like lightning.
Rainbows plunge into cesspools.

Maggots bask in sunflower stems:
Every beauty turns into slime.

In the crucifix circus of Rome, Plato lurks,
Persuading shepherds to rip apart sheep.

O, if only Heaven would heal the distress
Of the maternity morgue!

Children, fresh, get delivered, cheap,
To this slaughterhouse world.

And stars bend down, like scythes,
To reap vast harvests of tears.

Veil'd Devil

The garden's natural façade of sun
Shadows coffee—my own, my face therein,
As I surface, dark and bitter, from night's
Surfeit. My image here is counterfeit—
Cupped, puce, *coupé*, so cupidic Negro
I groan—like a *Negroni*—origin:
Drunkard, as boozy as Bozo. I know
I've won this face, this hand, in each café—
At dawn, with ache of alcohol—loco—
Black cave in my brain, vacant, caving in....
        I's 'Black'—Greek Jew by name (*George Elliott*)—
Chastise white paper with lashings of ink.
        I give myself guff: The creamed coffee shows
My buff-toned puffery. My typed face glows.

RED EYE

You know, it's very important to have long flowing red fingernails because red is passion.

TREY ANTHONY

"*Quemada!*"

à la manière d'Ennio Morricone

Love—yield love—while the body's ripe.
Don't ebb iceberg-like. Flame volcanic!
Wail as if a drum; never fall silent—
Save for wine-sodden sleep, uninterrupted.

Naked and aflutter in a four-legged bed—
With a coddling body opposite, gleaming,
The sun's never slight, never extinguished,
No matter how fat clouds crowd it from sight!

What good is chastity—if it's for good?
That lover, crumpling under caresses,
Is a saint, incandescent with sweat.
Jangle the bed! Shake it! Splash the wine!

"Fortuna"

à la manière de Piero Piccioni

I deposit, withdraw; she banks, profits—
Time's all we waste as we lay waste this night,
Lay siege to each other's seizing bodies,
And she incises seven inches deep,
As I size her up, our sighs redoubling
As our thighs mount, dismount, add, and subtract—
Multiple sums until our division.
A Great Depression frames the aftermath—
Depletion, deflation, what's left over—
Discredit, repossession of ripped pride,
The blank sheets, the stolen kisses, the loss
Of self, the taxing, maxed-out bankruptcy....
Yet, all we are—our total—counts for naught,
Unless we give everything in spending.

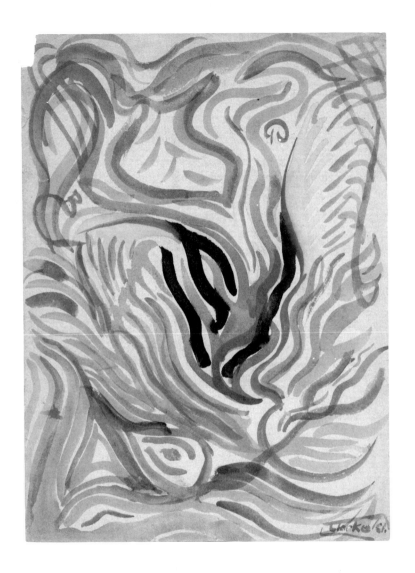

"Matto, Caldo, Soldi, Morto ... Girotondo"

à la manière d'Ennio Morricone

That bed, that night, that moon, her kiss, nothing
Felt bland—not even by a playboy's randy
Standards. We aroused splendour—me
And that white woman, in green grass, with red wine,

Spending, spending, agog, joyous, spending—
Foaming to a finish that could spring up
Genesis—the human revelation.
Our lips were not angrily impatient;

No, they had to bruise and to be bruised—grudging,
Thus, an arid eternity gaped between each kiss.
We supped on *Gato Negro*—*vino rosso*, tasty fire,
That flared a lusty candle in our bellies.

We could practise congress, let gaiety
Leave us winded, but wound in our four arms,
Love levitating us above filth—
Even if the grass was staining us.

"Blues for Big Scotia"

à la manière d'Oscar Peterson

Oui: I parleyed half-sugar, part-vinegar,
Played a baroque vagabond, scheming
A saintly orgy, a feel-good idyll,
Like a peacock strutting—gamely—in mud.

But I was smitten by that smear of radiance
Where I was kinked in the inky grass,
A cod aroma tingeing fingers, while she and I
Sculpted two apostles, prone, in wet earth.

In that damp swamp, that sea-wind,
Saw-grass dump, while rainy surf surged,
Our kneeling pleasures, our spasmodic rhapsody,
Discredited all kiddy pleasures of hotdogs and pop.

Did we feel coldly astonished—
Or dissident and reckless—
As we rocked to rapture, rococo,
Cocky, in that precocious April?

No matter: Confusion was on—
Juices squirting out everywhere—
And four eyes were squinting real hard
As breath partied in—and parted—our lungs.

"Eva La Venere Selvaggia"

à la manière de Roberto Pregadio

Our fingers mingled; our tongues twined, twisted;
We writhed; we snatched at each other; we sighed.

I had to grapple that rippling, skittish mist;
My torrents had to burst her ice, scald her flesh....

Kisses unfolded like—like—a spreading plague.
(I felt conspicuously—concupiscently—hard, not one bit vague.)

Her purse needed filling—but not with gold,
No, with spanking black iron, stainless, and bright.

"Ballade"

à la manière de Piero Piccioni

Black ink irradiates
Unspeakable letters:
Elsewise, this page looks
As dull as ice.

Against her blank skin,
I flap a blanket of rubber silk—
A velvety torso—
Smooth as tar, a black cologne.

We blaze and smoke—like two ants
Baked by a boy's magnifying glass.

Venal honey—
Shadowy apocalypse:
Black brogue gasps, snorts—

White paper, buckling, shouts!

"Intimità"

à la manière de Nora Orlandi

Syrupy politeness ends;
A peppery rumpus starts:

Not gingerly, but gingery,
The voluptuous tumult smells.

Slither:
White negligée angles down white skin.

Limbs kink and unkink—
Reptilian, snarling.

White sheets undulate eel-slippery.

But unambiguous hardness chinks
Soft marble, taps lacustrine dew—

Or tears—
Nicks.

Next, *Demerara* rum careens into *Carrara* marble.

"Un Po' D'Ironia Acida"

à la manière d'Ennio Morricone

Grim eagerness rams us into bed,
And—fast—we rampage, trample, like horses.

Dark, dour Alpine inches impale that pale
Abyss, bliss upon bliss, jostling, shaking....

A crow as despoiling as a black tornado,
Thus I become, inch by inch, an angel,
Pure black sinew and pinion
Bolting her white-hot core, that box-sliver.

Like two seminal animals in heat,
We plagiarize *Love,* tart it up, fake it.
We fuck like we're digging each other's grave—
Or like two vipers—in a rut—rutting.

Back-and-forth, to-and-fro, in-and-out, then:
Sultry result! A rainy pus—that sap of light!

"Fine Della Missione"

à la manière de Bruno Nicolai

Openness of that clasp!
Cunning, liberal fecundity!

Great, sweet song of silk
Riding under rough fur!

Lush drapes—
The folds.

Come, black pumps, see-through black stockings,
Show a naked rump,

Bring the open cleft,
That eye, eyeing,

And set up for a soaking—
This suave grave:

My Negro organ exults, milking,
Blanching, that sugary cavity!

To the Muse

à la manière d'Irving Layton

Let us meet in cities of refuge and of poetry,
Where you, learnèd, turn shameless as an animal,
Though there's sculpted marble under your clothes,
And your colour is as opulent as snow.

Let your kisses blaze my skin, already exuberant gold
Next to your vehement, diamond masterpiece,
And let me be topaz gilding your pearl,
My bronze stylus driving us to a honeyed *opera*.

Si, let us make love and sip filario.
Let's not talk a lot of guff.

Ah, once more, my sweet, to your embrocating kiss!
Once more, to your intoxicating ardour!

RED LIPS

Remember when we used to eat Seville oranges
sprinkled with salt from the Swahili coast
dive for pearls in the Red Sea,
bloom roses from the red soil of the Rift valley?

AFUA COOPER

I Loved You Once†

I loved you once; thus *Tranquility* quails;—
Rabid *Love* harries still my flesh and frame.
But, darling, let no cyclone havoc your sails,
For, though I'm hurting, I bear you no blame.

I loved you recklessly, in pure surrender,
Welcomed sorrows, jealousies, black and blue.
A love as intense and intent and tender,
God let another lover render you....

† *Pace* Dudley Randall's translation of Alexander Pushkin's
Russian verse.

Love Elegy Sonnet

à la manière de Pablo Neruda

Obliged to forget your olive waist,
Two breasts so gold the sun turns gold in turn,
That shimmering imperium—your sex,
My cup culminates with blood-crimson wine.

I sin, I rot, I'm torn, my little heart:
Dun, not docile, you won't be coaxed, and so
My dolour surges, unmediated.
Til gilded dawn, your beauty havocs me.

To you, I would be having—*behaving*—
If you would be giving to me, *chère* dame,
And let my lilting tongue lay you guiltless.

Please don't aggrieve me further! Let me plumb
The parade of your flesh, its plum fathoms,
For jasmine pursues you where you step.

James Brown's Rhetoric

Think!
I'll go crazy.
I know it's true.
Baby, you're right:
I've got to change.

It hurts to tell you
I got the feelin
I've got to cry.
Don't let it happen to me.
Please, please, please.

It's a man's world:
I got you
Bewildered?
I won't plead no more:
You're mine, you're mine.

I'll never, never let you go.
You made me love you.
It was you.
There must be a reason:
You've got the power.

Try me—
Prisoner of love—

24-Syllable Song

A little bit of this,
A little bit of that—
One hundred times to kiss
Each honey tit for tat.

First Light Blues

My daily, raisin bread
Demands my weekly wine.
My daily, sugar bread
Breeds my weakness— *that* red wine.
My knife sinks in butter,
My tongue drinks up brine.

God knows there's no honey
Like that liquor twixt your legs!
God knows there's no med'cine
Like that cure-all twixt your legs!
I slurp it all straight down
And fill it when ya begs.

Blues, gal, be chokin us—
Tears be smokin in your eyes.
Blues now be poundin us—
Tears be drownin your two eyes.
But blues still got me goin—
And comin twixt your thighs.

You're fickle cos you're young,
But you better treat me nice.
Doncha dare say I'm wrong—
Justice is fire, not just ice.
Gal, stay all the night long,
We'll make the sun rise twice.

Tomcat/Pussycat Blues

Heard a wild tomcat growl....
Some lil pussy just screech.
Tom caterwauled so damn much,
Po pussy had to screech.
Their racket rocked so raucous,
Even midnight got no sleep.

Each dog and bitch got barkin:
Each backyard heard complaint.
Doggone bitches howled so loud,
Neighbour served neighbour complaint.
But puss caught sweet martyrdom:
She purred just like a saint.

When animals fall in heat,
Their morals chew the dust.
Critters just ain't civilized:
They creep nude, dawn to dusk.
And us varnished varmints
Lend arm and leg to *Lust*.

Let pussy scratch and mewl,
Tomcat ain't feelin hurt.
Let pussy bite, hiss, and howl,
Mistah Tom ain't deterred:
He hounds pussy *sans souci*,
Licks pussy for dessert.

Marcia

à la manière de Chet Baker

Remember your lilac perfume the rain only magnified,
Your kiss like baked apples—cinnamon all over,
And the orange curving of your tensed thighs,
Your body, hot and insolent as July.

Remember the merciless rose in your black hair—
And the black hair of your *lord-have-mercy* rose—
Cola-sweet, cashmere-soft, cocoa-scented.
We snoozed under stars that were … gold earrings.

Now I awake to stars like dried-up sunflowers,
Finger thorny words in spotlit darkness.

Marcia, whaddya mean
You distrust these metaphors?

Bellissima mia,
We had another way of speaking …

When we were honest.

Sestina: April

After gods, we surrender to lovers,
Seeking beauty that always satisfies,
To revel in sunlit obscenities,
Every gay April, in the spring tumult,
To engage in creamy crimes—
An ivory music, as indestructible as sunlight.

Something there is about April that satisfies—
Even if one suffer physical obscenities
Like those that drive priests to tumult
And exultation in the filthiest crimes,
Those conducted far from sunlight
In those murky lairs reserved for lovers.

But holy are the bedtime obscenities
Where lover pitches lover to a tumult,
Spicing bland sins with sugary crimes,
In moonlight, dawn, and even April sunlight.
Thus, lovers actually behave like lovers,
Having each other until the other satisfies.

Nature, in April, floods in tumult:
Its white churn washes away crimes;
Its clarity is like water and sunlight,
The ideal assemblage for real lovers,
Who only turn away once love satisfies,
Once they have tasted joyous obscenities.

In April, the young commit no crimes,
But are as clean and honest as sunlight,
And love each other as blamelessly as lovers,
Discovering, like saints, the ways sin satisfies,
Excusing each other of any obscenities,
While each one milks a tidal tumult.

What is the month of love and sunlight?
Ask all those who play April lovers!
For thirty refreshing days, it satisfies,
All those poets of obscenities,
Who find passion a physical tumult,
And conceive kisses as delicious crimes.

Tell all the lovers that April satisfies,
That its obscenities mount a glorious tumult,
And that all its crimes dissolve to sunlight.

Old Man

(*Pace* Marot)†

Cold now, gone nights of playboy riot,
When my hot kiss sparked gals ablaze.
Now, April's dead, August's quiet,
And pains chill once-fire-hearted days.

Sweet Eros, youth's idol, I gave you
Everything, and God knows it's fact.
I'd serve you now—if I could have you—
Priapic faculties intact.

† *Pace* Babette Deutsch's translation of Alexander Pushkin's
Russian verse.

RED SEA

and our blood
is red, red, red
life
energy

ANDREA THOMPSON

North is freedom

North is freedom—
Uptown, down-home:
Each book a drum;
Each life a poem.

Going to Halifax

à la manière de Gregory Frankson

If you are going to Hell,
I, I, am going to Halifax—
where cars giggle at accidents along vermicelli streets,
and poxy doxies snarl, "Get yer ass out here, gal!"
Citizens watch crab-like things copulate
in the lewd grass of the Commons,
or undertake tearful screws in homemade brothels,
moms and dads looking on, clapping.
          Stores stack *Schwartz* spices
(so salty lovers reek of pepper),
'diddle' mags placed at kiddy-eye level,
with 'cancer sticks' as pretty and as mint as candy,
but also 'Newfie steak'—i.e. baloney,
Québécois *Joe Louis—Vachon* cakes—
shoe polish on a slice of bread—
hydrochloric-acid-blackened sugar,
Minard's liniment, and ten-seconds-gone lingerie,
and newspaper pages slathered
with mackerel guts and blood.
          In my sea-choked, Venetian-venereal city,
pearly gulls skirt purling waves,
purring girls go click click click
in tiny skirts, by the fat harbour,
or round bout the legislature,
while the wheezy buses break down
with boxers' seizures and sailors' syphilis

(because them idiots think ya can't get it
if ya can't spell it, eh?).
        "HFX" be unchaste, salubrious voices,
pigeon squawk and seagull chatter,
porn poetry,
and a line from *Othello*
adopted in a lollygagging room,
where suicide is the only rent,
and razor blades work the same miracles as nooses.

Address to Tomorrow's Negro Haligonians

Down home, you who haunt Gotti'gen Street,
And congress at the Derby and the Tap,
O, you who still call me "Georgie,"
Am I still your poet?
        I thought my poems should be boisterous
So the shouts would reach you,
O saintly, belovèd readers,
Through centuries of dust and lies.
        For all I know, as you read this line,
My hand is already an archaeological artifact.
Or, maybe, you Africans of Halifax
Are long gone back to Africa—or wherever.
        You remember when Downey was assassinated
And everybody owned a psycho Doberman Pinscher?
Do you remember my big, buck-toothed smile,
My Cornwallis Street Baptist Church Maoism?
As I write these words, it's officially April.
        What day is it now? What century is it?
Does my pigment still bleed through my poems?
Do you still love to guzzle *Alexander Keith's*?
Do brown kids still make snow angels in that empty Sobey's lot?
        Maybe Halifax has been long sunken under the waves
And the Yankee flag's single star represents every human.
Today, though, green leaves glisten amid the rain of birdsong,
And you ebon queens of the Ladies Auxiliary put on kilts.
        Perhaps all I love will have passed completely away
By the time your eyes read me.
        Tell me, does the night still come in, starry,
And the moon, blustery?

Four Unknown Women

As the maps declared, "Halifax, Nova Scotia,"
as the calendar read, "December 6, 1917,"
as the clock ticked off, "9:06 a.m.,"
as the crash subsided,
as a coward captain and crew scrambled for shelter in Dartmouth woods,
as the silence split with a black explosion,
as the *Mont Blanc* vanished and the *Imo* flew aground,
as the *Niobe* firemen burned or drowned,
as air grew heavy and sank in fire,
as molten iron rained from a suspected-Zeppelin-infested sky,
as windowpanes became daggers,
as the ocean moved in its bed and blanketed land,
as the telegraphs fell to jabberwocky,
as the schoolchildren wept and the churches collapsed,
as trains tipped over,
as funereal smoke umbrella'd ruins, ash, and torn-off, scattered limbs,
as the crushing of men and metal stopped,
as the blizzard blew blue cold over the left-over lives,

after the thunderclap of devastation—
after the slaughter of the city,

four unknown women—
black women from the flattened shantytown—
no, village—
Africville—
"for coloureds only,"
stranded behind tracks,
donned winter clothes and shoes and huge black overcoats

and went out into the snuffing-out snow,
looking over their losses—
ten of us,
the Seaview African Baptist Church—
and kept on stepping, unbent,
strong-willed,

to rebuild.

Taxi

They were not wrong—blonde mother, blonde daughter—
To laugh: Their dark driver dazzled; he jested
Wantonly, was jauntily seductive.
Courteous, cordial, proper, politic,
He lavished wit impeccably impish,
Encyclopedia-posh, and polished—
With scholarly asides and rhymester's timing,
Prompting the ladies' yielding gaiety,
To be repaid, he could hope, *handsomely*,
With a healthy tip (that common homage).
  So when their courtly, coppery chauffeur
Claimed to have a poet-son, it seemed *cute*.
But his passengers were polite enough
To transmute their blithe doubt to nods and smiles,
To giggle privately, at homecoming,
At the audacity of their driver,
To expect *them* to credit *him*—a hack
Operator, despite his suave grammar
And stunning puns—with fathering a son
Who could credibly be crowned a *poet*.
  He never knew their laughing disbelief,
Which was fair, casual, and jocular fun:
As far as they knew, men whose livelihoods
Are step-and-fetch-it stereotypes—black chaps
Delivering white ladies and luggage
Delicately to the appointed address—
Are not expected to sire any bard.

I heard their apology for this apt
Assumption, almost tearful, but tactful,
As I taxi'd a book into their hands,
And spoke almost as graciously, graceful,
As my unparalleled father would have.

RED SKY

Remember that redness in sunlight,

That perfume that filled the wide open
Museum of your days and nights.
How you thought it would never end.

FRED D'AGUIAR

Poor Imitation

*Why should some motherfucker make me feel bad
because of their ignorance?* MILES DAVIS

In Québec,
A snow-haired, sand-faced man points
At my sandalled feet, and asks,
"Do you speak Arabic?" I answer no.
He holds up a plastic bag, says "Shoes,"
then singles out my *pieds noirs* again.

In South Carolina,
at a roadside diner,
the blonde waitress guesses
I am
Japanese, or
Filipino, or
Brazilian, or
Chinese.

In Istanbul,
I am Malaysian.

In Havana,
I am, ecstatically, Cuban,
though my Spanish sounds English, word-for-word.

In Canada, I am comfortably
American in every café,
but suspiciously Arab at every airport.

Among African Americans,
I am African American,
okay?
But my accent's "weird."

These confusions?
Chalk it up to my brown face
and mish-mashed English,
mucking up black-and-white states....

Revery on the Kahlúa Bottle Label

for Nalo Hopkinson

When I sound *Kahlúa*, that *licor delicioso*,
I tour a diorama
of yellow sky and pebbly piazza,
spy a sagging palm tree,
dark-brown, penile, almost scraping
the roof of a Bauhaus-curved, yellow-brick,
two-storey building.
    Naturally, I thief the sombrero
of the drunk *amigo* dozing just inside
the brown, rococo archway
(the shape of a keyhole
that defines the scene:
the Aztec pyramid-like building
and the brown outline of a cloud—
the shape of a torn arm muscle,
blocking any vision
beyond the mid-point).
    I don that sun-stabbing hat,
and then I pirouette boldly into
the desolate, gold-scorched village,
all its shapes defined in dark-brown—
including that of an *amigo* astride
a horse—or a donkey—or a camel,
their shadows hennaing
the yellow ground....
    Entering the square—
a space out of a spaghetti Western—

with that squat, weird building on my right,
its lower windows and doors
styled vaguely Arabian,
I realize, somewhat drunkenly now,
the scene I'm in
isn't Mexico after all,
but, rather, Saudi Arabia.
      Certes, that anonymous aboriginal figure
is a decoy,
planted there to entice me
into this yellow-gold, volcanic chasm,
where I can be whipped
for public drunkenness
and have my right hand chopped off
for theft of that sombrero.

"Decisione"

à la manière d'Armando Trovajoli

When you jet on down to Basque Biarritz,
You and your wallet willingly go splits,
Where the Atlantic flows in starts and fits,
And spirits are spruced up with a lime spritz,
And bikinis look best as two teeny bits
(Glamour dazzles—gaudy—doubled with glitz),
And you are as pleased as anyone gets—
In a disco gyring to a 60s blitz
Of hot soul (during which no cripple sits),
While young girl moans and her paramour spits—
His hands all over her pert, perky tits,
And lovers groan until the starlight quits
(With manly pegs cementing female slits
Or plumbing tongues strumming so many clits),
And sex acts mimic tragicomic skits,
And each bull snorts and each flighty quail flits,
And wild water flails, wails (losing its wits),
At the Grande Plage, where each wave hits and hits
And foams and froths in sand craters and pits,
While the lighthouse beckons sombre poets
To unsheathe *un stylo* as time permits—
And scribble epics that croon like sonnets
(*The Apprenticeship of Duddy Kravitz*)....

At the Casino, cashing in her chits—
Spy B. Bardot, then those Kennedy shits,
Then pasty, slumming, Sorbonne "lit-crits"

(Some of them are twats, all of them are twits),
Plus film stars, fading (each one a ditz—
Confusing Australia and Austerlitz),
Leaving behind extreme close-ups of zits,
Waistlines gone haywire, careers on the fritz....

Make sure you quaff *Pelforth* (*brun*), never *Schlitz*—
Unlike Yanks—and Yankee-wannabe Brits.
(Canadians come with camouflage kits:
Each murderer croons, each assassin knits;
And Tories bed down with pinkos and Grits.)

This poem recycles the beginning: it's
"When you jet on down to Basque Biarritz...."

À Bellagio (III)

Above mountain-brushed water,
the sky turns so on-and-off chilly,
Italia, usually sun-stroked, feels
just like *Nuova Scozia*,
that brilliantly gloomy Latin Hades.
      Plunked under olive-shade, grape vines—
and *lapis-lazuli* grapes overhanging
a hung-over carafe of yellow-white wine,
I take ten thousand drags of this plonk
until my afro tenders ten thousand tarantulas.
      Five years gone, I sat here in Pescalo,
by this mountain-unscrolling water,
and scrawled "À Bellagio,"
while a man screamed at his dog, "Basta!":
I's still a black bastard bastardizing English.
      There is no freedom outside *Poetry*,
and its monarchical black ink,
dictating what's what and what ain't.
What any poet offers be
language set to music, then set free.
      See light diving in slanted salvos, ovals,
scuffing, buffing, the olive grape leaves.
Being as blind as a photographer to what ain't visible,
how must I picture interpretation,
but as an imagism of feeling?
      Wasting everything to glittering waste,
the day unleafs, its gilt flakes off,
in leaden, pewter darkness.

Plus a shadow-dragging dog arfs
at flapping, fleeing ducks.
      Slowly, the moon overtakes mountained lake,
its pulsating ivory like white wine—
amid so much *cassis*,
while I feel the fluctuation of impulse
among these forty lines of verse.
      Let me order a *Negroni*
(*Campari* plus vermouth plus gin)
as if the yelping dog
were a sign from God
that black is the soundtrack of white.

Rhodes: A Romance

the wind out of Rhodez
caught in the full of her sleeve
POUND

Sun-god island, home of winds
Toothed with March bite—
Sharp as the daggers that perforated,
Or winded, Caesar—

To poets, you are wholly Yeats' tower—
A cold, stony refuge—
Especially that hilltop home
(Not yet discovered by The Gideons International

Little Red Testament), where writers—
More into Sappho than Plato—
Garnish fat octopi with obese lemons
Or hold bottles of rose liqueur

As if Hamlet hoisting Yorick's skull.
Who goes here, if not
Slender, splendid women with cigarettes,
Or guys who celebrate absence

From spouse and home with absinthe,
And answer anxiety
By contemplating the gold-leaf moon
While sucking back draughts of Lesbos

Ouzo?
Cosma conjures up this pleasant exile:
Waves swish a beach
While ink swishes cross a page;

The wind snaps at branches; snags hair;
The wind is as stubborn as wine is supple
Or a kiss is subtle....
There's the smell of smoked fish

At Pericles' democracy; the look
Of a man grasping slyly a woman's hand.
Everyone is alone; many are lonely;
So we dream of unions that'll never end.

At the residence, ivy clamps on stone,
Green encunts grey,
Laundry and palm fronds
Whip or rustle in the wind,

While the wild cats prance,
Then pounce on offerings of tuna,
Milk, yogurt, or else
Recoil with disdain from our puny

Human gifts. In Rodos,
After black coffee sugared with gossip,
After chatting with L.—
A singular woman exhaling the Aegean—

You take to the ever-present beach,
Hear pebbles scrabble and crunch
Underfoot (a sound like breaking
Glass or promises),

Tread a scaly strand of shells,
Then pad cross sand
That's soft as July,
And come up on Durrell's house,

The Turkish headstones, breaking
Or broken, under eucalyptus,
Out back, while you brood
On the hard work of words,

The even harder work of love,
And you scrounge up wave-buffed
Stones, among the special coral
Of driftwood and seaweed.

By the time you complete your trek,
Sun-sodden sea surrenders
To moon-scorched night,
And beer-dizzy, after stopping

At the eccentric Chinese-Greek restaurant,
You pant uphill to the UNESCO abode,
While watching houses and hotels,
Some abandoned, burnt-out, or half-finished,

Topple into bottomless fathoms.
Thanks to Flavia Cosma's advice,
And wanting to leaf further into my novel
Manuscript, to find its roots,

I came to Rhodes, two years after
Her march (March MMV),
And discovered the blast of rain
Upon shutters,

The drizzle of coffee in the machine,
The benefits of an ouzo diet
Or strolling among ruins
(A *memento mori* hobby)—

But also sparking songs and conversations
In homemade Esperanto,
While pretending to be
A Marxist wino that only likes red wine,

Or claiming to have
A heart of bread, honey, and fire,
Or applauding translation
By ladies who have searing eyes

And serious clothes....
Suddenly, 28 days are history:
There are the beauties of goodbyes—
Embraces, then promises

Almost never kept, for they are
As wishy-washy as the wind
That rouses and serenades them into being.
But your work is done; half a rainbow

Leaps past your window;
Sadness
Mixes with business:
Packed bags, passport, cash.

Now the wine is finished;
Music sighs into silence.
What is left?
Wind, words—

Another form of love.

Touring the Historic Gardens, Annapolis Royal, Nova Scotia

à Aurélia

Summer comes into its own:
Each flower overcomes objections.
Though unwanted, undaunted mosquitoes flock,
haunt me and my daughter, A., now 11,
while we stab at ideal photo *topos*.

Look! A brook bucks gainst its stone channel.
Lily pads shout green fluorescence,
muting cowardly yellow light.

I repose in a darkening bower,
frame A. who poses
lovely in undiluted sun.

A dragonfly glitters above
pink-and-white *nénuphars*.

A. wants to go one way,
I another.
For now, she follows me.

She says, "The garden is beautiful,
most beautiful."
She's that age—
when beautiful things *are* unreservedly beautiful.

From an observation deck—
planked among pines and spruce—
we survey the warbling marsh
and the obsolescence-defiant, Acadian dykes.

(Is that a magnolia tree—
plagiarized from Longfellow's *Evangeline*?)

I slap fruitlessly at indefatigable
and deceitful mosquitoes
(dishonest hedonists),
occupying every glade's bit of shade.
They appear shadowy, vague,
but drill away like any hectoring lecturer....

The wind along the dykes
("*Les digues*," translates A.)—
mixes sewer stench, plus wild rose perfume—
and the smells of mud and grass, naturally,
thanks to the Annapolis River
stewing here in the Bay of Fundy....

A. forges on ahead of me.
Soon, I will follow—
as desperately as my father pursued me,
trying to hug me close
before *Death* pulled us apart,
though I, refusing his mortality,
just kept striding quickly away....

The antique railway bridge—
totem, factotum—stands stoic,
a mess of green paint and brown rust,
though more panting now than rustic.

We stray out onto gravel
that leads us beside unstill water.
See an orange-pink crab,
terminated,
scrambled up with charcoal-coloured stones.
A whirlpool dips in homage to a drainage pipe.

A. teeters on wet rocks; I steady her:
How many more times—
before all she has left
are memories to hold?

We ramble among *Phragmites Communis*—
elephant grass (fine for thatching).
A. is sleepy, but wants to espy the roses—
crimson not to be missed!

I pass under Dragon's Claw willow
(*Salix Matsudana 'Tortuosa'*):
It lets down tendrils
as straight, wavy, and unruly
as A.'s own hair.

In the new, tourism-crafted, Acadien log-cabin,
I plunk into an 'old' wooden chair;
A. dons clogs and clops about.

Outside our retro domicile,
homely vegetables—
still deeply rooted
(carrots, potatoes, beets, spinach)—
sprout pioneer dishes of soup and salad.

Now I've just nixed a mosquito.
(No, make that two!)
But the accomplishment—if satisfying—
is painful:
I also feel the sting of my slap!

(An artist has annexed the garden,
has anchored Bay of Fundy driftwood
within a circle of Annapolis River stones:
A Druid sundial.)

A. portraits another pond.
Crows flash overhead.
A dragonfly plays helicopter.
The Empress tree leaves mimic lily pads.

Now come we mid the roses—
red, white, pink—
an acre (at least) of them,
plus others pale, purple, and yellow,
and some as scarlet as poppies.
The drugged air reeks of tea and opium.

Some roses flare like carnations.
Others—the most aromatic—
bristle with studs—buds—of thorns.

(Where mosquitoes have dickered,
docked me blood,
the pain pricks.)

I navigate the Rose Maze,
ablaze with *rosa rugosa*,
and I fear I've lost A.

But, suddenly, she emerges—
copper Venus....

(I lose grasp of things,
but I want to seize *Joy*.)

Do I like the pallid roses best?
The Chicago Pink Peace hybrid tea
looms large and deeply open—
like a flowering birth canal.

In the Knot Garden,
lilac leaves laurel my head:
Who can untie complexity
until it is naught?

Apples are roundly commencing.
A bird cries the alarm:
"Summer is ending!"

Our camera is also exhausted.
All our images now are haunts.

A. steps on ahead—
into a bower—
like a bride.

She checks a map, sights an exit.
I pause under an appreciable apple tree.

She returns.
We stroll into the *ex* cathedral light.

Notice the Japanese Stewartia....

Its blossoms separate,

fall,

intact,
to the earth,

and flower still.

RED STAR

Red shall be the colour of the night
the red of the fire that shall burn the plains
and the red of the blood and anger of humans

AFUA COOPER

Casualties

January 16, 1991

Snow annihilates all beauty
this merciless January.
A white blitzkrieg, Klan-cruel,
arsons and obliterates.

Piercing lies numb us to pain.
Nerves and words die so we
can't feel agony or passion,
so we can't flinch or cry,

when we spy blurred children's
charred bodies protruding
from the smoking rubble
of statistics or see a man

stumbling in a blizzard
of bullets. Everything is
normal, absurdly normal.
We see, as if through a snow-

storm, darkly. Reporters
rat-a-tat-tat tactics,
stratagems. Missiles bristle
behind newspaper lines.

Our minds chill; we weather
the storm, huddle in dreams.
Exposed, though, a woman,
lashed by lightning, repents

of her flesh, becomes a living
X-ray, "collateral damage."
The first casualty of war
is language.

Parliamentary Statuary (*Viewed West to East*)

Flies roost upon Pearson's genial bronze.
So big, so rotund, so still, are they,
The insects mimic the prim, roly-poly prime minister.

Look at Queen Victoria, neo-Negroid now,
Her Latin inscription melting away—
Much like her Empire did.

Over here is Diefenbaker, defiant, sprightly,
And as weighty and indecisive as a Supreme Court jurist.
(In 1975, his blue eyes carved into my brown eyes
While I stabbed pink salmon in the Parliamentary Restaurant.)

At the Commons rear, find Thomas D'Arcy McGee—
Poète Assassiné—sculpted falling,
With blood—frozen lava—spurting from his chest.

Now observe Élisabeth Deux, thoroughbred sooty,
Straddling a black horse, a cape fanning behind her,
Masking the stallion's non-shitting rump.
(Posed thus, *Ma'am* is truly an Iron Lady—
Unlike when she dresses our stamps, coins, and cash.)

The Fab Five Femmes of the Persons Case
Stage their own life-sized, tea-party revolution:
Their empty cups tear up with—what—ether?

Sir John A. MacDonald towers—or totters.
One hand grips glassless spectacles.
No wonder: his eyes goggle, blear, alcoholic.

William Lyon Mackenzie King, bronze *martelé* outcast,
Casts a mottled, pitted, haunted shade,
Though his face glares, razor-smooth—
As arch and as severe as Fascist architecture....

Finally, catch Wilfrid Laurier—Peeping
"*Oncle*" Tom—
Peeking into the Château Laurier's careless bridal suites,
Unparliamentary....

Looking at Alma Duncan's Young Black Girl (1940)

à Viola Desmond (1914–65)

Her pose conjures Rodin's *Thinker*,
but is so naturally fetching,
no artist can leave her
to the mercy of *History*.

See: She's as slender and pretty
as the gal who'll be crowned Lizzie II,
whose pops—Georgie—chain smokes secretly
as London blazes under the Blitz.

It's 1940, y'all:
Europe is marble and manure,
stained glass and blood stains,
hot excrement of words shoved into Nuremburg faces.

Here in our provinces, these various Siberias,
under the cardboard eyes of George VI
(whose bro, ex-king, has a yen for Herr Hitler),
all is grey—the dull tint of a Mennonite Hell.

How to position a young black girl—
her dark, ochre excellence,
beauty like coffee—
pungent and exhilarating,

against the cool, mercantile air of Upper Canada,
the sour, brackish harmonies
of ministers of finance as dour as S.S. men,
if not quite as murderous?

(Bay Street considers *Art*
the mini-rectangular etchings that back each buck—
those portraits of negotiable wilderness—
forests, sawmills, pulp-and-paper,

custom killing in a slaughterhouse,
fire crackling under stars....)
The artist—Alma Mary Duncan—asks,
How came you, girl, to be here,

so womanish—
your two brown legs set off by those miniscule-heeled, black shoes,
and your upper body clad in that pink dress with the blue-ruffle scallop-nec.
then graced by that light brown jacket,

all enthroned on a beige pillow
atop an olive-coloured bedspread?
There is cause for wonder:
Our subject can't nurse the sick, not yet.

Is this her interview to be a maid,
to slave, 'in-service', in Rosedale?
What is in her purse (unseen)?
Tissue paper, cough drops, chewing gum, a coin pocket

brimming with pennies.
Does painter Duncan tell herself,
"Negresses are so much stronger
than we white ladies"?

Maybe.
But any resemblance to other women
who suffer like her is purely casual:
Painting is lacquer to insight.

Duncan's brushes—
oil on laminated paperboard—
testify her model shows
elusive and changeable:

Cotton plays contrapuntally
against the girl-woman's copper skin.
(Ain't she a smoky black gal,
her limbs all sheen, or pure music?)

Dismiss ideology of etiquette:
Snap fingers to the blues;
don't give a damn for any thin tones!
Yeah, vent volcanic hymns that singe the lips!

"Where is she from?"
Nay: Where she is from,
slave masters fell down in dust and fire.
Pigtails and licorice compose the diet.

She has a big, black, fearsome Bible;
she is a little tough, even hard, on the outside.
Her language is as sharp and piercing as a sword—
A piquant jolt of schoolbook English

and schoolyard slang.
Olive On glistens in her sable hair.
Her world isn't poetry
(Negroes can't afford that yet); it's potatoes.

She's not expected to finish school.
So, she's delinquent in the library.
She's got to char and chore—
to bring back a little meat.

In the British Methodist Episcopal Church,
pleasant beauties, in sumptuous, peacock silks,
pick up the Bible to put down the ugly.
Charcoal of words, ash of paper:

That's their Holy Writ.
Witnesses brandishing Bibles guard the gates of Hell
to keep out Th'Elect:
Their realm is power, judgments, and damnation—

women weeping awful songs.
Alma Duncan's young black girl—
our principal—
surely rests one hand on a radio dial,

while brooding over a book.
She's studyin jazz lingo—
to backtalk and lindy hop with
dem rude boys who throng—

like moths—round lampposts,
desperate to share in her body.
There's one scratchy-voiced, Baptist choir lad,
tuning his car engine like a guitar,

rapping a lying intimacy,
those ready-made, hand-me-down canticles:
He wants her to go with him
until he goes on his cologned way.

Say she's caught twixt blacks
who want her to succeed, but hope she won't,
and whites who expect her to fail,
and fear that she will.

So? She remains all beauty ever to be known—
spiritual and skin and onyx stone.
(Now that she has her *Liberty*,
don't she got a right to wax majestic?)

The hog we duly slaughter
and turn to bacon?
Too often, it's our dreams:
Tragedy of *Reason*, comedy of *Emotions*.

The All-Star Coloured Singers croon.
"God is Freedom,"
Malcolm X positively shouts—already—from the grave.
There is no accidental lyricism.

Miss A.D. doesn't mope in darkened galleries;
she crams her eyes with watercoloured light;
and serves a fat tea—
a broth that wallows on the tongue

(butter cream wrestling with maple syrup).
The young black girl swallows.
This potion renders her larger-than-life, Amazonian,
ready to be Rosa Parks or become Angela Davis.

Here is Duncan's signature of crayon and ash:
It is lightning of prophecy.

RED INK

Better read
Than dead.

Pushkin

T' imbibe Pushkin's *Evgeny Onegin*
Requires more than just one vermouth-gin

Negroni, that mixed-breed drink that's a moth
Aflutter on the tongue—but behemoth

Squabbling in the belly. Ain't Pushkin's verse
That blanchingly, indelibly perverse?

A white-faced Black Russian, and vigorous—
Verse as rigorous as a "nigger" is—

His taste is tricky, sometimes truculent:
Truth cannot succour if too succulent.

Other poets wax best in a museum
Where they aerate errors, *ad nauseum*.

But Pushkin mints candy out of *Candour*—
Rudely bittersweet or sour, sickly dour.

Pound: The Weigh-In

Only Pound amounts to Pound.
Yes, add up the negatives,
Then subtract the minuses,
And there's nothing left but
Light.†

† Night.

À *Irving Layton* (*1912–2006*)

The day you died, warring T V s screamed
Passionate, dreamy, amoral fashions.

A clergy of white spooks, puritanical eunuchs,
Resentful of your Shylock opulence—

Your plush thunder, your platinum-gold-silver physique,
Your Israelite currency of classical *chutzpah*—

Rang out their *Vices* virulently: They believed
Your biblical roar had ebbed to babble, then blackout;

That nullified, mummified, you'd fallen
As mute as chopped-up instruments,

That you had spelled out everything
That meant nothing,

And had begun to vanish into the finish,
The harsh varnish, of infinite *Criticism*.

II

But *Poetry*—yours—trumps *Prophecy*
And erases mundane, scruffy poets—

Those ad-exec purveyors of fads and moods,
Who confuse their larynxes with their assholes,

And also all the critics barking back and forth,
Their alphabet keys going yelp, yelp, yelp....

Never yackety, never yapping yinkyank,
Your voice hovered over *Love*, canting,

And sang of the stars—all their lusty,
Natural, blazing oxygen.

III

Holocaust instilled your *Wisdom*:
You heard fists smash through crystal,

Saw corpses belch black smoke of flies,
A raw white moon gleam like revealed bone,

Unholy Roman mechanics construct death,
'Jerry' engineers make it work,

Quack doctors, wielding real scalpels and knives,
Chaperone well-bred children to execution,

So Jews—mortal diamonds— shattered
Under Nazi jewellers' ordered hammers.

IV

You sang out of Montréal's textbook ghetto,
Streets adrift between messiahs and maggots,

Uncensored horse dung festering in novels,
Skeletal, white-lamé whores shoutin *joual*,

Market oranges smiling back at the sun,
Slaughtered pigeons birthing happy worms,

And self-elected saints synthesizing sin, then
Concocting tearful inundations of confessions.

V

In that era, all leather was alligator.
Each ecdysiast peeled off silk like smoke.

You wanted a gal, unilaterally kinky,
One looking like snow but as hot as an inferno,

Some Leonard Cohen-sculpted, lyrical beauty,
All marigold hair and chlorophyll eyes.

You learned that wedding bonds pull taut—
Tighter than any noose

(Whose fit is as just as *Lust*)—
And yet, no woman stays as close as a wound....

Defying Canada, this faux British colony
Of swamps and glaciers and mosquitoes,

You yelled *"Mazel tov"* in Montréal,
Murmured *"Ciao"* on the Mediterranean.

The Eliot-recommended Pound
Recommended Ol' Possum Eliot,

But you followed A.M. Klein,
Occupying *Eternity*.

Thus, Hebrew-Yiddish-Jewish Romanian,
English-chanting, solar-singing Canadian,

You will outlive the living
And outwit the dead.

V I I

From the dark Bastille of *Literature*,
You rise, blazing, sun-bright: Messiah!

À Derek Walcott

Victoria harbour looks tar-brushed foam,
Or it's diamond-studded tar, residue
Of that snooty empire—Britannia,
And its parliament, that seraglio,
Whose sooty copy (though squat, faux-Hindu,
A Sphinx) is lit up now—like a Klan cross....
I've jetted here to worship a poet—
The West Indies' celestial papyrus—
Among provincials, false, blanching, their eyes
Blue—like sulphur, catching fire. But Walcott
Weathers each shadow's sombre light, triumphs,
Yes, over *Death* too, so black ink blazes
Or ignites darkly dazzling words, flared stars,
Black holes—staggering, dizzying, to sight....

RED ARSENIC

The last thing you want is to work in
the Red areas where life is hard....

MAO ZEDONG

The Most Lamentable Roman Tragedy
of Titus Andronicus

for Gérard Étienne (1936–2008)

Squalls of rusted trumpet and busted sax.
Tribunes and Senators promenade a staircase
Of white marble steps and chrome railings.

Enter below Saturninus and his psychos at one door,
And Bassianus and his cutthroats at the other,
Hefting big bass drums and sanguinary flags.

Marcus, from a balcony, hands down the gemmed crown.
Exeunt his Soldiers, craving rum as strong as oysters.
Havoc of trumpet.
They storm the Senate House to slurp wine.

Enter a Police Captain, Irish, liquored up, cussing.
Queen Tamora, glittering, kneels.

Exeunt Titus' sons with Alarbus, a nobody, invisible.

Tamora, a glimmering cockroach, rears.

Rally the Boys of Titus Andronicus again.
Squawk saxophone, then deposit a gleaming coffin in the tomb.

(The columns of the Senate—
Like columns of numbers—
Hide columns of soldiers.)

Enter Lavinia, lithe, vinegary virgin.
She vogues her way towards the throne,
But spurns the tattooed Emperor's drooling.
He sighs spitefully.
His glazed-eye gaze drags cross her teats.

Spy Marcus now, sullen, brooding, downstage.

His saffron robe makes Saturninus glow in the dark.
Laurels instantly style him Caesar.

A long excitement of piano ensues.
Titus' sword and prisoners are gifted to Saturninus:
Leeches, sows, accountants (his harem), all sing.
Boom brass trumpets and tom-toms.

Exeunt omnes—except Aaron the Moor.
Sound of fingers popping.

The Andronici slide one hacked-up son into a marble sheath.
Their tempers grind against each other.

Blast Marine Corps trumpets.
Exeunt all but the Moor,
Him giggling at "Whitey."

Come forth Titus Andronicus and his three breathing sons,
Four celestial profiles facing glory.

Hear hounds, then horns, in a dinning peal.

Arrives Aaron, alone, as usual:
The traitorous black intellectual with the moneybag.
He vows, "Bassianus will be two sadists' sieve.
Lavinia will see her mouth spouting blood."

Soon, Bassianus' baritone pleas dribble into his beard.
Two fraternizing swords dice him up.

Next, Tamora's cunt-hunting sons snatch up Lavinia.
Quick, she is bare-assed, spread-eagled.
The uppity bitch ingests two obscene spikes at once.

Demetrius and Chiron carnally enjoy Lavinia,
Spunking her sex-thing,
Atop fiancé Bassianus's draining corpse.

Lavinia sobs, pukes—humiliated.
But her brotherly rapists put boots to her again.

Malicious honey spurts cross her face;
Some drips snottily into her puckering anus.
Her voice croaks like a spitted hog's.

(Yes, she'd clawed and snarled and spat and bitten,
But had only pissed off the twin rigid buggers,
Who writhed upon her—like lice, colonizing her skin.)

After actually shitting on Bassianus,
Demetrius dumps the well-punctured now-feces-smeared corpse
Down a sewer.
Chuckling, the boys exeunt.
They tug the girl by her dugs.

Plummets into the gash, another Andronicus.
Plops into the slash, another Andronicus.

Saturninus' bootlickers haul Quintus, Martius,
And the skewered Bassianus from the abyss.

One sword's hacked him open from anus to nape.

Lavinia cleaves her mouth,
The ashamed oval of her lips,
And red ribbons fly out.

An iguana—dark sunlight—drizzles across grey stones.

Intrude the Tribunes as Judges, plus the Senators,
With Titus' two convicted assassin-sons, Quintus, Martius,
Chained and shackled down like death-row killers.

They pass to the execution oasis—
A guillotine, fly-jewelled skulls jumbled about—
With Titus running alongside, begging, fawning,
"Saturninus, spare an old soldier's sons."

Enter Lucius with his sword held aloft.
Impotent, he kneels.

Impotent, Andronicus lieth down.
He flails like a fly on its back.
And the dour, scornful Judges pass him by.

Aaron, grinning, chops off Titus's hand.
It twitches, then fists.

Lavinia weeps, kneels, collapses,
Still red in mouth and wrists and thighs—
Red like that sink of grief, the heart.

Appears a Messenger with two Andronici heads,
Still improbably blond, and a fire-charred hand.
Sets down heads, that bump across the table,
Fall, bruising, on the red-tile floor,
And sets down a scorned, charcoal hand.
Exits.

Lavinia bends, kisses those lopped-off heads
With her lopped-tongue mouth.
Lavinia and Titus pledge some appalling purpose.
They kiss as only they can: a pact of knives.

A fly alights on the reject hand.
Marcus deems it the black symbol of Aaron,
And stabs the fly with a knife,
And stabs into Titus's dead hand.

Lavinia overturns a heap of drab tomes.
Titus, disturbed, helps her:
They up-end all that useless poetry.

With a pool cue, Titus carves his gal's name in sand.

Lavinia plops the stick in her mouth,
And guides it with her stumps.
Achieving refreshed literacy,
She spells out her violators.

She pictures how two pricks had her pinned.
How their steel wool scraped her race and sex.

Aaron, Chiron, and Demetrius penetrate one portal,
And at the other door, sight aroused Lucius,
With a bundle of arrows with verses inked thereon.

Black brass peals, black copper night echoes.

Nurse prances in with a blackamoor infant.
Aaron unsheathes his blade and seizes his heir,
Queen Tamora's royal prince.

He jabs the Nurse through her breast,
Impales her like a rat.

Exeunt nauseated Demetrius and Chiron,
Lugging off Nurse's gore-spewing body.

March in Titus, angry Marcus, terrifying Lucius,
Leading a posse brandishing bows.

Titus grasps a dozen poem-poisoned arrows.
He arms his backers, who shoot lustily.
"What is *murder*? Just a trochee."

Enter Emperor Saturninus and Empress Tamora
And her two quivering sons,
Ideal prey for cock-scalding schoolgirls.

Saturninus reeks of ostentatious fornications—
Doggy-style, often with sows.

Tamora, Cleopatra-like, tongues her lips.

Saturninus brandishes in his hands the arrows
Titus' Trojans launched his way.
He cusses, "They swear out verses against my eyes!"
He fucks off under guard.

Troops in a Goth, in chainmail vest,
Leading Aaron with his babe snug against his chest.

Another Goth, in khaki, brings a ladder, which Aaron,
At sword-point, is pricked to climb.
A third Goth places Aaron's child on the ground.
They will prod Aaron to fall upon his infant son
And his sword simultaneously.

Instead, as Machiavellian as a banker,
Aaron bargains:
"I'll expose the dainty conspiracy,
The jokes of crime,
That cut the Andronici to exquisite pieces,
Just cradle my perfect son."

Agreeably, he is borne from the ladder.
He is shackled like any nigger with a dagger.

Bravado of trumpets, saxophones, guitars, drums.
Black flags and black horses descend blackly upon Rome,
Imperial abattoir.
Smells of tar and smoke singeing the air.

Tamora's sons knock, and Titus, aloft, with papers,
Unlocks his library door.
Their faces dazzle with guilt.

Quickly, the boys are beguiled, bound, gagged,
And strung up by their heels in the kitchen—
A Mussolini and a Petacci.

Appear Titus and Marcus with a cleaver,
And happy Lavinia cradling a basin.
She gestures, "Dearie, the works?"

Titus opens the pale throats of Tamora's pups.
Violent quivers quake their draining bodies.

Exeunt omnes with the two cadavers—
Throats split like vaginas.

Now blustering Saturninus and Tamora, bristling with guards,
Bust into Titus's home.
Trumpets guffawing, a table is plumped up.
Here's Titus, regaled like a cook, placing the meat dishes.

Glides in Lavinia, nun-like, black veiled, stately,
Her tart tits shivering her thin, taut shift.

The meat reeks pinkly of pig.
It is tasty, savoury, and Tamora chews peacefully,
Devouring her sons like they deflowered Lavinia.

Titus, jovial, unveils the *Mona Lisa*-like Lavinia,
Whose smile digs a red well.

He knifes her as he tongues, one last time,
That mouth like a rose—dewy, petalled, and thorny.

Before anyone can do anything,
Titus stabs vomiting Tamora, in her eye;

Saturninus thrusts his sword through Titus.
In sweaty consummation.

With an axe, Marcus smacks Saturninus's face.
Mashed, shamed, with steel slicing his forehead,
That hole in his head almost goes straight through.

The Goths clatter in and corral Marcus and Lucius.
The royal guards, pacified, await news,
And Marcus says everything,
Just by pointing out Aaron's bawling, mixed-race babe.

Exeunt the healthy from the diseased house.
Exult, some guards shouldering Emperor Marcus.

A long crisis now of trumpets, foxily nervous,
As the murderous Andronici descend.

Old-fashioned, dreamy, Marcus kisses Titus.
Lucius kisses Titus, opulent murderer.

The white moon skirts darkness;
Light drops to the earth and dies.

The ocean pierces the beach:
Daggers of water plunge home.

Summon Aaron under needling guard,
Demanding his son, his infant boy.

His crucifixion is spat out, fixed up,
But his son is swaddled and nursed.

Exeunt omnes with the corpulent, imperial cadavers
And the superb, martial dust—
To be blazed with tears, then fire.

Finis the Tragedy of Titus Andronicus.

Malcolm X: The Last Interview (February 21, 1965), with Vogue (via James Baldwin)

I

Race is a masque—
brown, in my case;

and it's a mosque—
blue, in *our* black case.

In my opinion,
the Slave Trade was like Hiroshima.

(Yes, sir, evil done 24/7
ain't evil anymore,
but *professionalism*!)

White man lives like a ship floats—
buoyant,
forgetful it gonna sink one day.

Why reproach me my realism?

Every self-portrait is *nature morte*—
an apparition of bones—
no matter how much champagne
sparkles like chandeliers:

Our mothers birth us into morgues.

Onto blank TV screens I strut,
Lincoln-lanky,
a bleak, apocalyptic beatnik
in the dull garb of a hangin judge,
spouting annoying poetry—
"Hate"
(conspirators say I orate).

No, no: I'm a man
as astringent and brilliant
as detergent:
Out to recast the outcast Negro,
make him (and her) black,
then even blacker,
but clean—
so that we prove as demoralizing to the white man
as sunlight is to filth.

Yes, I make words cuss on paper,
concuss in air.
Enthralled radios crackle like sandpaper.

I am but what I give:

A voice of fire
born from solid rock.

(Every orator or writer
gotta mete out scorching *Truth*.)

No tongue of hesitancy!
The blues are my only language—
each elegant, crisp text.

Even my humour is a hammer
crackin noggins from the rear:

When brains bust out in whimsical, bloody blossom,
you see clear proof that minds are being changed!

(But it's always taboo to be too frank.)

II

How I started?

Elected class prez (hurrah, hurrah),
but stroked like a puppy.
Dreamt of handing down law;
got schooled that nigguhs pick up trash.

Slipped to Beantown;
conked out:
straightened my naps
so I'd copy icy guys in slick suits,
them shiny characters in zoots,
daddy-o.

Had to be a cool cat,
and get as high as a second-storey man.

On guitar nights, jazzy, sexy with carnival:
Scrambled to each dance,
gambled at romance.

Began to twirl Sophia—
white bitch with a deep itch
for black cock round the clock—

white pearls, like cum,
roping her neck,
even lacing her little black dress.

(She looked just like what she did—
and what she loved to do:
Charismatic slumming.)

Knew I'd either net that piece of ass—
or vend her a piece of my mind.

Told her: "Women here wear gaudy jewellery.
You don't need to.

"You're fetching—
just like a cold is catching."

A black-lace, pale vixen was she—
a panty-flashing gal—
liking every licking.

In our coloured, chequered love affair,
maple-and-cream,

there was a milky stink,
acrid as tar.

You should've seen
the stability of my dick—
like a fine horse—
studding!

No spring chicken—
no bird with its head cut off—
my quail would spread-eagle just as I liked....

(Cashiers, tellers, maids, all so pitilessly *lumpen*,
will easily marinate any hotel bed.)

Sophia kept me kept—
fox in her henhouse—

kept me narcotized too,

so I held my street-hustler credentials,

through our Russian roulette of French kisses....

Next, I barged into Gotham.

At Small's Paradise,
the cracker pervs
bought "blackbirds" with cherry mouths
and cheery caws.

(Mr. Small had a big, tall girlfriend—
taller than I am.)

I learned to thrive
where others throng—
round *Vice*:
numbers
(I don't mean verses),
reefer,
pussy....

(Everyone's *alma mater* is cunny.)

Lemme tell ya,
Vice is a lucrative doctrine—
lotsa moolah, dough, less chump change:

True even during that bloody, dirty War,
when blood-and-soil fanatics
crimsoned pages with atrocities.

I like New York—
marine, cosmopolitan city—
despite flagrant, cocksucker pickpockets
in flared skirts:

Still a great town for tackling
king-size, mongrel gals,
roped down and handcuffed.

(Recall Roxy—Mistress *Noire*—in leather toggery,
preaching, "My beauty you will worship; your ass I will whip.")

But New Scotland Arch
had a bone to pick with me,
cused me a tiefin from him

(his grey matter
was a-goin grey):

Said he'd kill me nigguh red,
slap me with a .44,
grass my ass under,
quite gangrene, dead.

A no-no.

Guys with no guts are sissies:

Vamoosed back to Sophia,
Beantown:
Came a cat burglar,

lured alluring cunts
"into the gutter"—

whined the judge
after I was hoisted
post-heist:

Black boys are posed to ride rails,
hot seats,
not classy-chassis chicks.

Judge squinted at a jitterbug jigaboo—
as comic, seductive, outrageous,
as a spotlight lit-up whore.

(Yes, I was a subtle burglar, sir.
I deserve, for that crime,
disfigurement from your mouth,
destruction by your pen,

but *Respect*, for a robber,
depends on who is robbed.

Damn me as a proficient delinquent—
as you like:
Fine—
I was never no *incognito* Negro.)

Jailed, I was Satan—
cussin, smokin, pork eatin:
The 'hole'—isolated—
fit my home.

Yes, I suffered the dirt and pain of imprisonment.

When The Honourable Elijah Muhummad
floated right on into my cell—
as sure as you and I be rappin right now—
he was impetuous, scintillating:
He seemed to have a secret knowledge of weaknesses.

He scolded, "Wake up, brother!"

I couldn't be a sobre-minded idler:
Gave up cunning passions
for passionate cunning.

Inked a slanting rush of a-b-c's cross scribbler pages.
Devoured dictionaries,
cannibalized encyclopedias, and

The Constitution—a diet of tears—
each page only a sheet of dirty snow.

Al-Qur'an means *reading* (*aloud*):
That's *al-qaeda* (*the foundation*).

Released,
after a Chicago pilgrimage,

I ventured into salacious New York—
town of verminous harlots,
ominous pricks,
voluminous cockroaches—
the electric chair as Pop Art—
Bauhaus curves in high-class porn....

Landed here the very same year
pubic hair got legalized.

There was a lot of loud, bad poetry by bongo,
goateed boys spanking bare-bottom 'cupcakes',
commies howling thermonuclear jingles.

Guys couldn't live on milk and bread alone:
had to have 45s—
black, slick jive,
plus a redhead in plastic, see-through shoes.

Radios screamed all night—
Lady Day, Miles....
They warned, "Beware the fat bully,
the fatuous believer."

Should've listened!

Stead, I strutted, got addicted
to being recorded, quoted—
turned an electronic junkie—

needing a 'hit' of microphones, cameras,
newsprint.

(Turbulent, black ink seas froth up
a savage, white spray: *Journalism*.)

Got good copy,
sold good blow:

My zingers zipped,
snatching headlines,
triggering a million headaches....

I speaketh: "The Atlantic is Africa—
liquidated!

"Rats jump rope with massa—
that criminal so crooked, he's got rickets.

"Like a vampire, impaled by a stake,
the white boy feels our knife at his heart."

Played I the scrupulous, sterile, raging, crypto-Fascist,
Hitler's carbon-copy monster,
noirist poet, Castro pal,
edgy excellence in wit:

I was black Jack Dandy,
a bizarre outlaw of words.

At first, I voiced propaganda's trifles,
or petitions in garrulous English,
harangues that were "Honourable" advertisements.

My voice beat raw, unclean air
until it screamed,
"Mercy!"

(I got no evanescent, shrinking voice;
I project pizzazz, sizzle.)

I corralled the Nation.
I shook up America:
"Don't make me so blue fucking mad!"

(Wed me a sister who wears a sunflower face,
whose glide is Cleopatra's,
who has brown-black eyes, black-olive hair—
and mirrors a Mediterranean Madonna.)

My speech, salted with spondees
and peppered with dactyls,
got converts feasting.

My polemics, as caustic as Cold War,
didn't spare even cutie-pie Kennedy,
that too-soon perforated candidate.

But, gee whiz, do pygmies ever envy *Success*!

Now, nuance insinuates
murmurs of murder from sallow men.

(The threats are not only threatening,
but extremely real.)

So, once Cassius signed himself Ali, I soared
back to Africa:
Palm trees, multiple, shocked me
with excitement of Egypt.

Each day, in Ghana, had its true poem—
or palm tree.

Now, I'm back in the U.S. cess—
unwilling to tread shit now.

III

Bejewelled vipers congregate,
ready fangs and venom,
alibis and photo-ops.

They buzz and hiss—
this unholy menagerie—
angry that their hustler *cum* prophet
('Lijah, illegit),
fucking, is defrocked;
or, defrocked, is fucking.

I'll make it plain:
Mr. Poole is a rustic bull
in his secretarial pool,
(a slave to his loins' diminutive giant),
and an adroit bullshitter.
A polite scoundrel,
a divine of difficulties,

he's as simple as a gutter.

Because this fact is spunk jetted in each fanatic eye,
I'm aggressively slandered—

even though the dossiers are everywhere,
packed with secret, dirty pictures—

in Washington, last gasp of Europe's
vanishing white supremacy.

But no amount of *paperasserie*
affirms my truth....

(Alas, a gymnast
is no match for a hypnotist.)

IV

Today's a fine, clear Sunday—
ideal for an assassin's aim,
an up-to-date death.

You may feel sorry for me.
Don't be:
Glorious—if gory—finales are constant.

Doves tumble from heaven.
Arrows protrude from their breasts.

Anyway,
the dead are comprehensively dead.

V

A salaam alaikum....

Next, a polka of bullets—
many shots—
screaming, crying,
chairs crashing, clattering....

Blood dripping from his shoulders.

VI

We were deaf until he spoke.
His voice was our lives.

(He only sought *Justice*—
that beautiful, austere *Charity*.)

He was all that we may now hope to be.

Charles Mingus: An Autobiography

for Ayanna Black (1939–2009)

In Halifax, plenty sobbing: Your birth.
A steam vent gasps under snow.
Dogs chuck vomit at strange crotches.

Preacher poses like a matador in the church.
Gospel songs—no bullshit—charge at you.
Each note reeks: tangy.

In North End Halifax—the Beggars' Quarter,
Light squeaks in as dim as nickels.
Insults clatter like chump change.

That absolute black gal bewitches!
You take to her your gross instrument,
And learn frenzy.

Jazz lessons with dark rum—
"Mmmmmmmm, well, uh huh...."
Fuck ideas.

Each sweet glass is a bidet.
Guzzle her like a washing machine.
Devastate like an architect!

No cash means
You don't dream.
Time to bust outta bed and gust outta town.

That Toronto, spectacular gal—
Crystal chassis, chrome ass—
Swishes light against shadows.

Play her like maracas—
Her big body, sombre, blasé:
Screw like a brouhaha.

Curious sweetness ensues:
Nightclubs and neon vibrate.
Sunlight arrives with the fresh air.

Garble arguments, misunderstand,
Be misunderstood:
Some bitch stabs at you with a butter knife.

Screams jangle like a tambourine.
Que sera sera.
Neighbours speed past like cars.

Ain't no locomotion in kneelin.
Re-adjust the sun, sponge-up tears.
Coffee clarifies a situation—and cash cleans it up.

Fashion a scalpel-keen suit—
Wave aluminum-bright cigarettes.
Pull off a *beaucoup* blues *coup*, suh!

Impudent gals, imprudent belles,
Tequila-fiery, wine-perfumed,
Got you shameless, fucking non-stop.

No whore's ass is unhappy.
You party just like comedians party—
Improvising, nervy.

Your voice oozes raillery, winks.
But distance is a fortress:
Being far away is just like being locked up.

Your state is practically psychiatric.
Being so far from Nova Scotia is like being
Walled up in the Nova Scotia Insane Asylum.

Interned black man, it's your turn
To suffer goddamn white supremacy—
White coats, straightjackets, shock treatments.

You feel like you've had a frontal lobotomy—
Black Nova Scotian in a blear, blank world—
Ink spot on Ku Klux Klan sheets—

Your black being trumpets as loudly
As words jetted onto paper.
Might as well glissando and growl, eh?

Precipitously, you free yourself.
Why defer tomorrow—
Or demur from today?

Snack on blondes—
Double-quick—
These creampuffs, these tasty cavities.

Cloture nails down possibility.
Barge ahead like music
Exploding through windows.

Break and enter,
But be extra elegant:
Your actions will shout like loudspeakers.

The new gal's red lips sigh out lies,
Slurp up silver, gold.... Man-oh-man!
Stuff her purse til you burst!

To puff on a Havana—
Even under a guillotine,
That's freedom.

Life's ridiculous otherwise.
Your muscles trouble critics;
Your graceful lope leaves them feeling leaden.

A virtuoso subversive, you ain't no mannequin,
No blow-hard, no asshole—
You are ice-cool, but snarl gunfire.

Your bass sounds like a typewriter
Punctuating *Ulysses*,
Or like a shotgun puncturing Odysseus.

Fools admire only their mire.
Diagnose it for what it is:
They splatter their brains through their butts.

Folly of years, you understand:
Anger serves art.
Truth is a razor blade, two wrists, a bath.

Stranded on this estranging planet—
Carved by a butcher, not a jeweler—
Where is there any real radiance?

The city is combat theatre.
The public voices trepidation.
You soliloquize anyway, despite crying.

Everybody's used to being pilloried,
Silenced, immobilized,
But you are as free as music.

Subtle blues, supple blues,
Let you push forward—with feeling.
So what if overseers suffer paroxysms?

Success is survival—
Applause of homeys, governors.
You go home to Halifax

To be swamped by love,
Then floated off by death.
You vanish into an Atlantic of earth.

But worms can't eat music.
It exists like light—
Up in the air, divine—

To be divined—
Like tears
Dissolved in snow....

RED TAPE

The rapes, the massacres, the violations and the tortures which
have reddened the African continent, Christianity wishes to
persuade the Negro to see as a legitimate chastisement....

"To the Poet" and, later, "Old Man (*Pace* Marot)" are my rewrites
of Alexander Pushkin (1799–1837) translations by Constance Gar-
nett and Babette Deutsch, respectively, found in *The Poems, Prose*
& Plays of Pushkin, Ed. Avrahm Yarmolinsky (New York: Modern
Library, 1936). My rewrite of "I Loved You Once," chases Dudley
Randall's translation in his *After the Killing* (Chicago: Third World
Press, 1973).

The "uta" is a Japanese verse-form that Ms. Winifred Hall, then
of Vancouver, British Columbia, brought to my attention in 2007
correspondence. It is a *tanka*—a brief lyric poem taking the typical
syllable count, parlayed over five lines, of five-seven-five-seven-seven.

"Other Angles." Cf. "I. i" in *Blue* (2001) and "IV. iii" in *Black*
(2006).

"Royal Audience": This poem is a fairy tale, not history.

"Veil'd Devil": *George* is Greek for *farmer; Elliott* descends from
the Hebrew for *man of God*. Cf. "A Discourse on My Name" in *Black*
(2006).

The "Red Eye" lyrics suffered a Byzantine genesis. In Istanbul in March 2003, I found a two-volume, Latin-English edition of Martial's *Epigrams*. Then, in Nova Scotia (ex-Roman colony), in July 2006, I read Petronius's *Satyricon*. In 2007, I reread Ovid and Catullus and Horace. The Imperial Romans shocked me because of their unholy (pre-Christian) dissection of sexuality. But 1960s & 1970s Italian pop music and screen scores—utterly sublime—effected a different seduction. I look to the Latin writers for license and to (mainly) Italian composers for titles. (Englished, the titles are, in order of appearance, "Burn!," "Fortune," "Mad, Hot, Rich, Dead … A Round Dance," "Eva, The Savage Venus," "Ballad," "Intimacy," "A Little, Acid Irony," and "End of the Mission.")

"James Brown's Rhetoric": This poem catalogues the early hits of Brown (1933–2006).

"Revery on the Kahlúa Bottle Label": The poem's subject is the label as it was in 2001. In 2007, Malibu-Kahlúa International, the Pernod Ricard-owned company, decided to 'refresh' the brand by dropping several design elements that my poem explores. Pity.

"À Bellagio (III)": Cf. "À Bellagio" and "À Bellagio (II)" in *Black* (2006).

"Touring the Historic Gardens, Annapolis Royal, Nova Scotia": Cf. "I. v" in *Blue* (2001) and "VI. i" in *Black* (2006).

"North is freedom": This poem's affixed to Doug Bamford's sculpture, unveiled in 2007, at the North End Memorial Library, in Halifax, Nova Scotia.

"Four Unknown Women": Writ on May 13, 1979, the poem eyes a photograph that appears in *Fire On the Water: An Anthology of Black Nova Scotian Writing, Volume One* (1991). See Negative 2451 in the James Collection, City of Toronto Archives, City Hall, Toronto, Ontario.

In "Taxi," the phrase "step-and-fetch-it," served, with slight deformation, as the stage name of African-American actor Stepin Fetchit (1902–85).

"Casualties": This poem pans media coverage of the Persian Gulf War of 1991.

"Looking at Alma Duncan's *Young Black Girl* (1940)": A City of Toronto-commissioned response to the painting (housed in the Art Gallery of Ontario), the poem attempts to recall the milieu of the 'sitting' of the subject and the approach to her taken by Duncan (1917–2004).

"The Most Lamentable Roman Tragedy of Titus Andronicus": Here is Shakespeare's 1594 play as plotted by a few eccentric stage directions.

"Malcolm X: The Last Interview (February 21, 1965), with *Vogue* (*via* James Baldwin)": This poem imagines that X (b. 1925) gave a final, unscripted, uncensored interview to novelist Baldwin (1924–87), immediately before the former's assassination.

"Charles Mingus: An Autobiography": This poem pretends that African America's great jazz bassist (1922–79) was not only Canadian, but Africadian. (*Negro* experiences transgress all borders.)

"17, 34, 51": Cf. Elton John, *11-17-70* (1971).

RED LIGHT DISTRICT

where are your flaming-red red-light districts
selling hot assorted worm-blown meat

AMATORITSERO EDE

These poems were written in Halifax (Nova Scotia); Saint John (Nouveau-Brunswick); Montréal (Québec); Toronto and Ottawa (Ontario); Edmonton (Alberta); Victoria (British Columbia); Durham (North Carolina); Chicago (Illinois); Playa del Carmen (México); London (England); Biarritz and Paris (France); Bellagio and Grottammare (Italy); Rodos (Greece); Krakow (Poland); and St. Petersburg (Russia). They were edited in Geneva (Switzerland), Berlin (Germany), and Black River (Nova Scotia).

The blue pencils, black marks, and red ink of Ama Ede, John Fraser, Marja Haapio, Linda Hutcheon, Cory Lavender, Liza Oliver, Joe Pivato, Andrew Steeves, and Paul Zemokhol bettered these poems.

Financial support emanated from The Pierre Elliott Trudeau Fellowship Prize (2005–8), awarded by The Trudeau Foundation, and from The E.J. Pratt Professorship (2003–), supported by both Victoria University and Dr. Sonia Labatt. I am thankful for their assistance, but also excuse them from any responsibility for my compositions.

Some of these poems debuted in *So Much Things to Say: 100 Cala-*

bash Poets (2010); *Sons of Lovers: An Anthology of Poetry by Black Men* (2001); *Canadian Literature*; *Malahat Review*; *Sulfur*; *CV2*; *Windsor Review*; *Tongue 7, Quill & Quire*; *Idea&s*; *Voices: Writers of African Descent* (1992); *Cantos Cadre*; *The Exile Book of Poetry in Translation: 20 Canadian Poets Take On the World* (2009); *Lichen*; *Sentinel International Poetry Review; Murderous Signs; Kola; Vallum*; *To Find Us: Words and Images of Halifax* (2006); and *Dalhousie Review*. "Forgotten Diatribe" is titled "IV. iv" in *Kola*, 13.3 (2001). "Royal Audience" first appeared in Todd Swift's blogspot (January 2011). "To the Muse" was translated by Marco Fazzini and issued on a 2009 postcard advertising the Commune di Grottammare (Italy). "Poor Imitations" ["Imitatii de Joasa Speta"] and "Pushkin" ["Puskin"], appeared in Flavia Cosma's Romanian translation in *Citadela*, 1.3 (2007); "Rhodes: A Romance" appeared in Cosma's *Postcards from Rhodes* (2010); "Pushkin" appeared in Marja Haapio's Finnish translation in *Parnasso*, 7 (2007). "Love Elegy Sonnet" first appeared (as "Elegia de Amor [Soneto]") in Cosma's Spanish translation in *Generacion Abierta*, 21.55 (2009). It first appeared in English in *Alhambra Poetry Calendar 2011: Poetry Anthology* (2010).

Re: The Art: My late father, William—Bill—Clarke, of Halifax, Nova Scotia, was, as an impoverished adolescent, apprenticed to a sign painter, a discipline that was his primary tutoring in art. At age 18, in 1953, he left Queen Elizabeth High School, in Grade 10, but not before executing a number of pieces (in crayon, charcoal, pastel, and watercolour) that I have since inherited. In November-December 1959, after losing his railway work, B.C. returned to art with a vengeance, mass-producing, *à la* Warhol, a series of painted scenes for sale (his self-employment, really). His technique was to pencil a design, then use Tester's model-kit oils to paint the scene *on glass*, and then position crinkled tinfoil between the glass and the cardboard backing of the frame. The results shimmered. Thus, B.C. sold so many pieces so quickly that he was, briefly, a successful commercial artist. But the railway rehired him, and then he learned he had a son (yours truly), and so he packed up his paints to settle into Coloured, proletarian-bourgeois respectability as a father, husband, and passenger-rail employee. Yet, some of my warmest memories of him honour his decision, in the mid-1960s, to make art again—using the oil-on-glass technique, but also exploring collage and other ideas gleaned from a single course of study at the Nova Scotia College of Art and Design. (My mother, Geraldine, once told me that B.C. quit art school because he couldn't take criticism. Probably.) My father abandoned his art in 1970 (not counting a few drawings he did later at my request). I'd always thought his experience unique. Then, I came across Bob Beatty's book, *Florida's Highwaymen: Legendary Landscapes* (2005), which documents a school of African-American artists, *floruit* 1950s–80s, all self taught men, who abandoned menial labour in favour of painting—not for "art for art's sake," but so as to prosper and live free. I wonder whether B.C. ever encountered any of the Afro-Floridians , either via the railway or on his motorcycle sorties to New England and New York City. Or did he figure out, for himself, that art *could* free an Africadian from the genial humiliations of a reluctantly bestowed, strictly stereotyped, and poorly remunerated j-o-b? Yes, I'm no art critic, but I believe B.C.'s art is good, and so it appears here:

page 35   *Heaven and Hades* (1961)
page 48   *Xmas Muses* (ca. 1958)
page 53   *Junior States* (ca. 1959)
page 78   *Sudden Instant* (ca. 1953)
page 104   *Native Son* (1953)
page 129   *Empire State Glimpse* (1972)
page 155   *George: Five and a Half Years* (1965)

(*Pound, Cornered,* on page 106, is by Anonymous.)

To stay any charge that I am blinded by simple, filial devotion, I will mention that *Ramble*, my father's painting for *Blues and Bliss: The Poetry of George Elliott Clarke*, ed. John Paul Fiorentino (2008), was nominated for an American, small-press prize for best cover art: Not bad for work accomplished 55 years earlier.

Word up: I am profoundly grateful to Andrew Steeves for digitizing and utilizing B.C.'s letters—his own font (drafted in the 1960s). Thus, *Red*'s title page and end papers debut what Mr. Steeves dubs, "Bill Clarke Caps." In my view, this rough-hewn, yet elegant majuscule typeface testifies to the nature of Africadian culture: Our art is *crafty*.

RED LIGHT

GEORGE ELLIOTT CLARKE
(1960–)

Son, brother, helpmate, father—
Friend, and poet: Thy Believer.

17, 34, 51

Two thirds my life a poet, I
Dream I am a burning shadow:
Gleam—like a portrait etched in lye,
Or ink. I scald paper, and cry
Atlantic tears (never for show).
Two thirds my life a poet, I
Deem each pen a distillery,
As when I started, drunk, aglow,
Gleaming—a portrait etched in lye,
Seventeen, and damnably shy
(One gal to 'pell-mell' my pillow).
Two thirds my life a poet, I
See I'm one, but still can't say why.
Now fifty-one, shouldn't I know?
Gleam like a portrait etched in lye!
A poet is his poetry:
Naked as ash, his words say so.
Two thirds my life a poet, I
Gleam—like a portrait etched in lye....

The type is Adobe's GARAMOND PREMIER PRO, a digital revival of types designed by the French punchcutter Claude Garamont (c. 1490–1561) designed for Adobe by Robert Slimbach.

This book was typeset by Andrew Steeves & printed offset and bound under the direction of Gary Dunfield at Gaspereau Press, Kentville, NS.

7   6   5   4   3   2   1

NATIONAL LIBRARY OF CANADA CATALOGUING IN PUBLICATION

Clarke, George Elliott, 1960–
    Red / George Elliott Clarke.

Poems.
ISBN 978-1-55447-098-3

    I. Title.

PS8555.L3748R44 2011   C811'.54   C2011-902123-4

GASPEREAU PRESS LIMITED ❡ GARY DUNFIELD
& ANDREW STEEVES ❡ PRINTERS & PUBLISHERS
47 CHURCH AVENUE KENTVILLE NOVA SCOTIA   B4N 2M7
Literary Outfitters & Cultural Wilderness Guides
www.gaspereau.com

Poetry

Saltwater Spirituals and Deeper Blues (1983)
Whylah Falls (1990)
Lush Dreams, Blue Exile: Fugitive Poems (1994)
Gold Indigoes (2000)
Execution Poems (2000)
Blue (2001)
Africadian History: An Exhibition Catalogue (2001)
Illuminated Verses (2005)
Black (2006)
Blues and Bliss: The Poetry of George Elliott Clarke
   (Ed. Jon Paul Fiorentino, 2008)
I & I (2009)
The Gospel of X (2010)

Fiction

George & Rue: A Novel (2004)

Prose

(Ed.) Fire on the Water: An Anthology of Black
Nova Scotian Writing. 2 vols. (1991–1992)
(Ed.) Eyeing the North Star: Directions in African-
   Canadian Literature (1997)
(Ed.) The Dalhousie Review. Special Africadian Issue.
   ([1999] 1997)
Odysseys Home: Mapping African-Canadian Literature
   (2002)

Drama

Whylah Falls: The Play (1999)
Beatrice Chancy (1999)
Québécité: A Jazz Fantasia in Three Cantos (2003)
Trudeau: Long March / Shining Path (2007)